Dartmoor pub walks

Robert Hesketh

GW00480643

Bossiney Books · Exeter

This updated reprint 2023
First published 2017 by
Bossiney Books Ltd, 68 Thorndale Courts, Whitycombe Way, Exeter, EX4 2NY
www.bossineybooks.com

ISBN 978-1-915664-03-7

Acknowledgements
The maps are by Graham Hallowell
All photographs are by the author, www.roberthesketh.co.uk

Printed in Great Britain by Deltor, Satash, PL12 6LZ

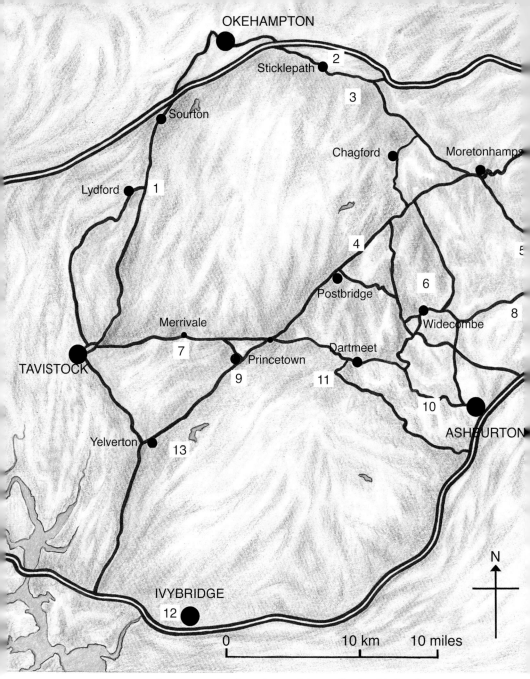

The approximate starting locations of the walks in this book

Introduction

Dartmoor is southern England's highest, largest wilderness, a walker's paradise. There is nowhere quite like it. Each rocky tor has its own unique profile whilst the marks of human activity from earlier times are everywhere, from prehistoric villages and stone circles to Victorian railways – though dwarfed by the heathery wastes and steeply wooded valleys.

All the walks have at least one pub either on the circuit or at the end. The walks have been selected for their own quality rather than that of the catering, but I hope you won't be disappointed by either. Please bear in mind that the more remote pubs are family-run businesses and may close one or two days a week, especially outside the high season. Check first!

All the routes in this book can be walked in a day, some in a morning or afternoon, though it is best to start with the shorter walks if you are out of practice. The time you need depends on how fast you walk and how interested you are in what you see – you might want to spend time watching a buzzard hunting, or exploring a historic church.

Safety (please take seriously)

Walking Dartmoor is safe and trouble free – if you are prepared. In the first place the weather can change suddenly. Wind, fog or rain can appear as though out of nowhere: the rain can be intense and the temperature may drop abruptly.

Please do not go without walking boots and suitable clothing.

Drinking water, map and compass, plus waterproofs and an extra layer are essential, as well as a comfortable rucksack. Many, including myself, add a walking stick, mobile phone (though reception can be restricted to high points) and food to the list.

The sketch maps in this book are just that – sketches. You should go equipped with the Ordnance Survey Explorer OL28.

Ticks are a potential nuisance, especially in hot, humid weather. Wearing long trousers and socks offers some protection against these tiny parasites, which may carry a bacterial infection, Lyme disease. If one does attach itself to you, remove it promptly and carefully with tweezers, being careful to leave none of it in your skin to minimise the risk of infection. Lock your car and don't leave valuables in it.

Access

Unenclosed moorland areas are generally open access. Please keep to paths over enclosed moorland, leave gates as appropriate and keep dogs under control.

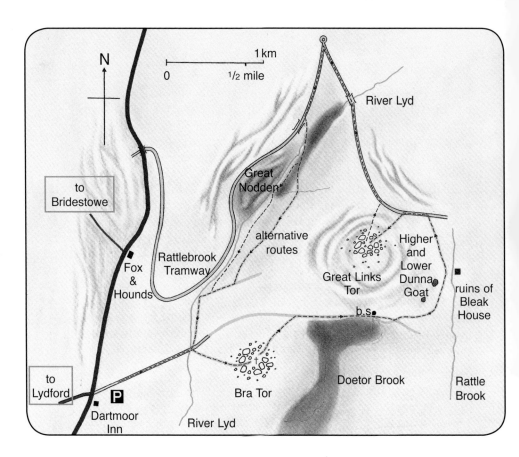

Walk 1 Great Links Tor and the Castle Inn, Lydford

Distance: 13 km (8 miles)   Time: 4½ hours
Character: Two steep ascents are rewarded with wonderful views.
Allow time to explore the interesting industrial remains from tinning
and peat cutting. Much of the route is on open moorland – wet after
rain. Map, compass and boots essential.

Start from the car park at SX 525854. This is 300m up a rough track
by the Dartmoor Inn on the A386, opposite the turning to Lydford.
The car park is just beyond the first gate.

Follow the track ahead from the car park, keeping the stone wall on
your left. An impressive line of tors faces you. Cross the infant River
Lyd by stepping stones or the adjacent bridge. Head east up the flank
of Bra Tor – also known locally as Brat Tor or Brattor, and given as
Bray Tor on the OS map – by the rough path, aiming for the granite
cross on the summit. William Widgery, the local landscape painter,
erected it in 1887 to celebrate Queen Victoria's Golden Jubilee.

Walk north-east from Bra Tor for 750 m, following a faint path over the turf until you strike a distinct west-east path. Turn right onto this old tinners' track, worn deep into the ground in places like a trench. The extensive overgrown workings to the south, especially around the head of Doetor Brook, give a vivid idea of how much rock Dartmoor tinners moved, mostly using hand tools in the pre-industrial age. Follow the track east, ignoring side turnings.

The treeless windswept beauty of the high moor opens out in front. Look out for a characteristic Dartmoor boundary stone ('BS' on OS maps) inscribed L for Lydford parish and BS for Bridestowe on its opposite face. Keep following the track east, ignoring any side tracks.

When you are abreast of Lower Dunna Goat, bear left. (If you reach the firing range marker poles you've gone too far! These warn walkers to go no further when the red flags are flying.) Follow the path NNE with two small tors, Lower and then Higher Dunna Goat, on your left. Across Rattle Brook from Higher Dunna Goat is the aptly named ruin, Bleak House, the lonely home of the West of England Compressed Peat Company's representatives. Six companies tried to make a success of digging peat here between 1868 and 1955. They scarred the land, but time has healed the wounds.

Walk towards the ruin, but don't cross the stream. Keep left along

the top of the left bank, then follow a distinct track heading sometimes north, sometimes north-west.

When you meet the Rattlebrook Railway, turn left. The rails have
gone, but the cuttings, embankments and bridges remain. It was built
to join the LSWR line running from Okehampton to Plymouth,
which is now, west of Meldon Quarry, a cycle route.

Just beyond the summit point, a peaty track leads up the left bank
of the cutting. This allows you to detour to visit Great Links Tor, an
impressive granite pile which is one of the highest points of Dartmoor
and, at 586 m (over 1900 ft), almost qualifies as a mountain. It offers
even finer views than Bra Tor. Return to the tramway and turn left.

Walk downhill for nearly 2 km, then turn sharp left where the trucks
used to stop and reverse down the next section. Continue till you
come to a bridge, at which point bear left on a rather indistinct path
heading south. Follow it down and cross the River Lyd, then turn right
along the east bank. There is no defined path near the river, so pick
your way carefully through the old tin stream workings. Alternatively,
there's a slightly easier route higher up the hill – see sketch map. Great
Nodden rises on the right, forming a small gorge. Composed of shale,
it marks the boundary between moorland granite and metamorphic
rocks to the west.

Recross the river by the stepping stones used at the start and retrace
your steps to the car park. You now have a rich choice of pubs. The
Dartmoor Inn lies at the end of the track. My publisher swears by the
Fox and Hounds, 1.5 km towards Okehampton, but my own prefer-
ence is the Castle Inn in Lydford itself, a mile ahead.

The Castle Inn, Lydford
01822 820241

Built in the 16th century, the Castle Inn was originally the home of the
keeper of Lydford Castle. It served as a farmhouse, and later as an ale
house too. It has many interesting features including three open fires:
the one in the restaurant is medieval and was taken from Lydford
Castle itself. There are exposed beams (some ancient) and slate floors.

Of particular interest are the Saxon pennies on display. A mint
operated at Lydford between the reigns of Edward the Martyr (975-8)
and Edward the Confessor (1042-66), when it was one of four mints
in Devon – the others being at Totnes, Exeter and Barnstaple. Many
early English coins, some looted by the Vikings, others paid to them
as Dane geld, are now housed in Scandinavian museums. It is some
satisfaction to know that our ancestors beat off the Danes at Lydford
in 997. This is commemorated by a plaque near the church.

Walk 2   Sticklepath, Belstone and South Tawton

Length: 10km (6¹/4 miles)   Time: 3 hours
Character: Mainly a riverside and field path walk, this route is full
of interest. Finch Foundry has working waterwheels driving various
machinery. South Tawton has a handsome church and church house.
This is a walk with, at the time of writing, three pubs – one at Belstone
and two in Sticklepath.
  Do not attempt the walk if the river is in flood.

Park in Sticklepath's main street, near the Finch Foundry (National
Trust). This 19th century forge and edge-tool factory, powered by
three waterwheels fed by a leat from the River Taw, is now a working
museum. There are regular demonstrations of the machinery, including a grindstone, drop hammer and tilt hammer. At the rear is an
unusual Quaker burying ground, recalling the early Quaker community in Sticklepath and the welcome they gave the Wesleys on their
journeys westwards. Walk downhill past the Taw River Inn with its
17th century date-stones.
  Cross the bridge, noting its boundary stone, and turn right onto
PUBLIC BRIDLEPATH THE MOOR etc. Follow the path alongside the river,
passing a footbridge, and go through a gate. Turn right, PUBLIC

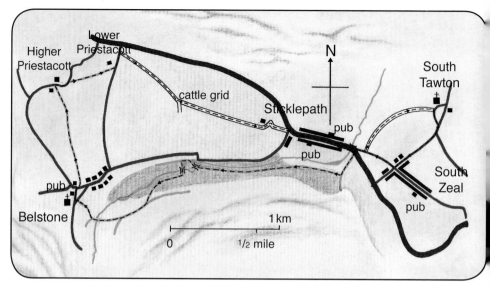

FOOTPATH. Walk on the bankside path past the old mill and the sluice gate feeding the leat for Finch Foundry. The path winds through mixed deciduous woodland, accompanied by the river's music. Moss and ferns grow thickly, testifying to the clean moist air.

Cross a footbridge carved with a quotation from *Tarka the Otter*. (In the novel, Tarka disputes a rabbit with Swagdagger the stoat.) Bear right out to a track and turn left. Follow the track for 100m then turn left to recross the river by the next footbridge. Turn right and keep to the path parallel to the river.

The path rises slightly and joins another path. After a while keep right and right again, to recross the Taw again via a footbridge just to the left of a ford. Keep right and steeply uphill, to enjoy a fine view of Belstone Cleave, reminiscent of Lustleigh Cleave (Walk 5).

Head for the centre of the village, dignified by its medieval church tower, and pass The Tors. This is first recorded as the New Inn in 1815, burned down and was replaced by the present building in 1896. Walk ahead to Zion Chapel – prominently labelled TELEGRAPH OFFICE. Turn right and after 30m turn left, PUBLIC FOOTPATH.

Keep the hedge on your right through two fields, then continue with the hedge on your left. Cross a stile and walk ahead as signed through a series of small fields, stiles and gates to a tarred lane. Turn right by Lower Priestacott.

Follow the lane for 220m. Take the second footpath on the right, TONGUE END. Cross three fields to a lane (just to the right of the pumping station). Turn left, and after 125m turn right, PUBLIC BRIDLE-PATH SKAIGH AND STICKLEPATH. This old track, once the main

highway from Okehampton, offers views onto Dartmoor and over the rolling hills of mid-Devon to Exmoor.

At a cattle grid keep left. At the end of the old track carry straight on down the main street, passing (or entering) the Devonshire Inn. Retrace your steps past the foundry and over the bridge. Fork left and after 50 m turn left (UNSUITABLE FOR MOTORS). Follow this green lane uphill. The tall granite tower of St Andrew's church, South Tawton, appears as you top the hill: it has fine carved altar rails and pulpit.

Leave by the lychgate, where the church, village square, and 16th century church house, with its large granite blocks and external stairs, make an attractive group. Walk ahead. Keep right (SOUTH ZEAL) at the stump of Moon's Cross, which directed travellers from North Devon to fork left for eastern Dartmoor or right for the west.

After 500 m, at Zeal Head Cross, turn right again for Sticklepath and retrace your steps up from the bridge.

The Devonshire Inn (01837 840626)

Intriguing and unspoilt, this is a 16th century thatched inn on the old Exeter road. Beer is cooled by water from the leat and customers are warmed by hearty log fires. Take time to explore the bar, parlour and snug. There are many curiosities including flintlock weapons, bread ovens, a ship's bell, a sea chest and a grandfather clock. The Inn has customer car parking.

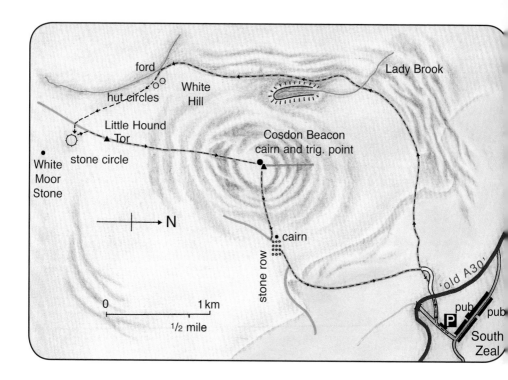

Walk 3 South Zeal and Cosdon Beacon

Distance: 12.1 km (7½ miles) Time: 4 hours
Character: Choose a clear day: the panoramic views of Dartmoor,
mid-Devon and Exmoor are superb. The prehistoric stone circle and
triple stone row should not be missed. Most of the route is on open
moor: parts will be wet after rain. Map, compass and navigational
skills are essential. This is a fairly demanding walk.

The Oxenham Arms (01837) 840244

A handsome granite and thatch building, the inn bears the arms of the
Oxenhams on the sign. Said to have been built in the 12th century, it
was recorded as an inn in 1477. Later it was rebuilt as the dower house
of the Burgoynes and then the Oxenhams. The snug contains a granite
menhir, perhaps 5000 years old. There are many other features,
including oak doors and beams and original flagstones.

Park at South Zeal's free car park (SX 652934). Turn right out of the
car park, up the lane. Fork right at 'Oakfield'.

Walk up to the main road (formerly the A30), cross and walk up
PUBLIC BRIDLEWAY. After 170 m, cut out a dog-leg in the track by using
the short cut (PUBLIC BRIDLEWAY). When the track forks, keep right.

Press on uphill (PUBLIC BRIDLEWAY) at the next path junction and continue uphill at the next two forks. Go through a gate and up an old drove lane. Keep following the main track to the open moor.

Then keep left twice, in both cases uphill on the stony track. (NB Do not divert south up Cosdon Beacon.) The track now runs parallel to a disused leat, and in time levels out, then descends to cross Lady Brook by a shallow ford. Sheep have created several minor paths.

Stick to the main path, which uses slightly higher ground at a little distance from Lady Brook, and follows the edge of a shallow tin-streaming gulley, then approximately follows the contour along a 'reave' – a long hummock which was once a field boundary.

You should be using your OS map here, but beware: it confidently shows a bridleway to Little Hound Tor but this is not evident as a path on the ground! Check your direction with a compass.

Continue with White Hill on your left downhill to a ford. Don't cross, but head SE through the heather, passing two hut circles. Pick up a rough path, which gains height steadily away from the brook.

Gradually swing from SE to S. Continue to a path junction. The Little Hound Tor stone circle lies just to the east of the track, 400 m south of Little Hound Tor, and the White Moor Stone (a Forest boundary marker) lies another 150 m from the circle.

11

Walk up to Little Hound Tor and follow the clear path ahead to Cosdon Beacon. This is one of Dartmoor's finest viewpoints: a magnificent array of Dartmoor tors stand south and west, and north and east the rolling hills of mid-Devon lead on to Exmoor.

Turn east at the triangulation pillar, which is perched on top of a massive prehistoric cairn, and follow the path down to the triple stone row – see photo above. At least 76 stone rows survive on Dartmoor, ranging from a few metres in length to over 3km. Triple rows are rare.

Stone rows and circles probably date from the Bronze Age, but perhaps even earlier. Their exact purpose is unknown.

The upper end of this triple row is well preserved. A peat track cuts through the middle of the row, and the stones actually extend for a further 60m, but most of them are hidden below the turf. Take the peat track, heading NE.

When the path forks, keep left and follow it downhill between dry stone walls. This sunken track is wet after rain.

Bear right at the next path junction and walk downhill. Ignore the signed PUBLIC FOOTPATH on the right. Continue downhill at the sign A30 AT PROSPECT. Walk on, retracing your steps to Hillfield and back to the car park. To visit the Oxenham Arms, walk through the car park and bear right into the main street. Turn left.

Walk 4   Warren House Inn, Lettaford and West Coombe

Distance: 14.2 km (9 miles)   Time: 4 ³/₄ hours
Character: A mixture of open moor and field paths, this superb walk
has lovely views and much of interest including a prehistoric stone row,
several longhouses and two ancient crosses. One long ascent towards the
end of the walk, one tricky stile. Map and compass essential.

Use the car park just to the east of the Warren House Inn (SX 676811), called the King's Oven – a reference to medieval tin smelting. Cross the road and walk up the steep gulley opposite: this is one of many mining scars in this intensely worked area.

When a rough path crosses the gulley near its upper end, bear right. The path gradually gains height as it heads to the Hurston ridge. Ignore cross paths. Keep left at the first fork in the path, then right at the next, and hopefully you will spot the stone row to your right.

Rejoin the main path and aim for the far north-east corner of Fernworthy Forest's boundary wall. The paths can be indistinct: if in doubt, head NNW to pick up the wall, and follow it along.

On reaching the lane, turn right along it. Follow the lane past Metherall and then for another 1.3 km to a cattle grid. After a further 70 m, opposite the entrance to Yardworthy, turn right onto FOOTPATH, climbing steep stone steps forming a stile.

Follow the field edge. Turn right at the next PUBLIC FOOTPATH sign along a track. After 150 m turn left at PATH sign. Pass through a small

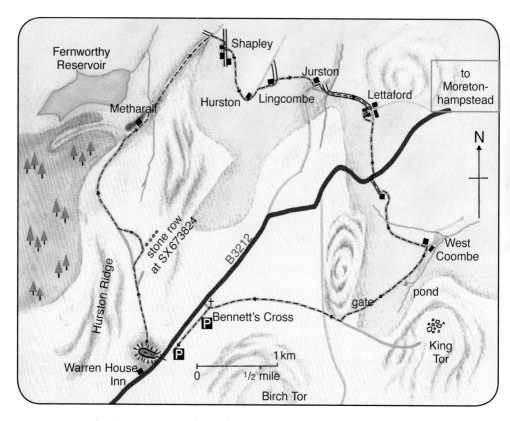

orchard, cross the stile and turn right as signed. Continue through a series of small fields to Hurston. Turn left across the front of the attractive granite and thatch farmhouse. Follow the lane for 230 m, then turn right MARINER'S WAY JURSTON. This is part of an ancient cross-country route used by sailors travelling between Bideford and Dartmouth.

Cross two small footbridges and turn left through a gate. Cross another wooden footbridge, pass Lingcombe farmhouse and immediately turn left, then turn right on PUBLIC FOOTPATH, through fields, heading east to Jurston. Reaching a lane, turn left along it and after 50 m turn right, PUBLIC FOOTPATH. Cross the brook and continue along the trackway to Lettaford, a typical Dartmoor medieval hamlet, originally of three longhouses. In a longhouse, the farmer's family lived at the upper end and the animals at the lower end, in the shippon below the cross passage. Turn right (PATH) then left after 50 m.

The MARINER'S WAY continues via yellow spot waymarks to the Moretonhampstead road. Cross over and walk on, MARINER'S WAY NATSWORTHY GATE. Leeper Cross is tucked away on the right of the

14

five-barred gate. Follow MARINER'S WAY signs around Moor Gate and then onward to WEST COOMBE. Here the path leads through the farm-yard to the magnificent longhouse. Divert 50 m down the lane to see the ash house: it is a circular granite building with a turf roof which was used to store household ash for fertilizer.

Retrace your steps, passing the longhouse on your left. Continue steeply uphill on the bridlepath. When the concrete path turns right, walk ahead as signed. Keeping the stream on your left, after a while you will pass old mine workings, including a pond. Continue up the well beaten path through the bracken – or in winter, if the path is unclear, head for a gate on the skyline.

From the gate take the minor path (grandly known as the Two Moors Way) which heads west over the brow of the hill and descends to a lane. Cross and continue on the well beaten path over the brow of the next hill, descending to medieval Bennett's Cross. Follow the path through the heather and parallel to the road, to the Warren House Inn.

The Warren House Inn (01822 880208)

At 434 m (1425 ft) above sea level, the Warren House Inn is the third highest in England. It was built in 1845, replacing the New Inn, which had stood on the opposite side of the road since it was turnpiked in the 1770s. Its name comes from the nearby rabbit warrens, dug to keep local tin miners in fresh meat. The sign depicts the 'three rabbits', a motif found in Widecombe church and elsewhere in the area and erroneously called the 'tinners' rabbits'. According to Tom Greeves and Elizabeth Stanbrook in their book about the inn, the animals are hares and a pre-Christian fertility symbol.

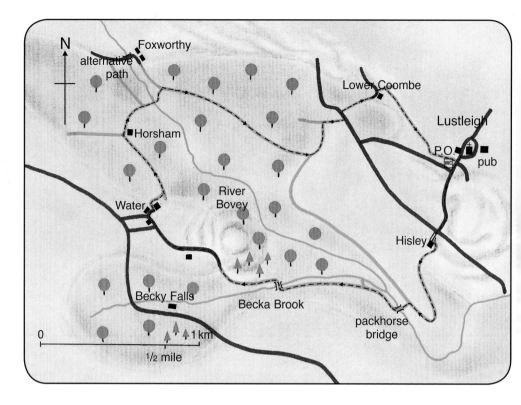

Walk 5 Lustleigh and the Cleave

Distance: 9.25 km (5³/₄ miles)   Time: 3 hours
Character: A woodland walk, starting at the pretty cob and thatch
village of Lustleigh and exploring both banks of the River Bovey, as well
as its tributary the Becka Brook. We cross the Bovey by a packhorse
bridge and re-cross by huge tumbled boulders. Parts of the route are
steep and can be muddy and slippery after rain. A delightful shady
walk for a hot day.

The Cleave Hotel (01647 277223)

The 15th century Cleave Hotel derives its name from Lustleigh Cleave,
which comes from the Old English *clif,* a cliff or bank. It was originally the main building of Lustleigh Farm, becoming a hotel in the
1920s. The splendid fireplace with its oak beam and bread oven was
discovered in the 1950s. Both bars have log fires and the flower-filled
beer garden is a delight. There is a good collection of period photographs, including Lustleigh Station and Lustleigh May Day.

Park in the centre of Lustleigh (SX 785813). Facing the Post Office,

turn left towards BAPTIST CHURCH. Cross a small bridge and walk ahead for RUDGE. Ignore side turnings and at Rudge Cross walk ahead PUBLIC BRIDLEPATH BOVEY VALLEY. Follow the path around Hisley and into the valley, where recent felling has opened out good views over Trendlebere Down. The path doglegs right.

Walk on down, then take the second track on the left to meet the river at Hisley Bridge. A typical Dartmoor packhorse bridge, it is just wide enough for the strings of packhorses that served moorland villages and industries before wheeled transport came into use here in the late eighteenth century.

Cross the bridge and walk ahead to a five-barred gate. Turn right, MANATON. At the next path junction do not cross the wooden bridge: walk ahead, PUBLIC BYWAY. Cross the Becka Brook at the next (stone) bridge and go through a gate marked WOODLAND TRUST – WELCOME. Here the Woodland Trust is currently felling conifers of low habitat value to encourage native trees to regenerate. Follow the track up to a junction with a PATH sign.

Walk on uphill on the main track, climbing steeply and ignoring side turnings. Continue ahead at the next path junction by a notice-board.

The path ultimately levels off and becomes a lane. When the lane divides, either divert left for refreshments at the Kestor Inn, or bear

right, PUBLIC BRIDLEWAY. Reaching Water Mill, turn left along the bridlepath. Turn left at the next junction, signed MANATON (INDIRECT) AND HORSHAM FOR FOOTPATH LUSTLEIGH CLEAVE. Ignore side turnings and follow the path past Horsham, following a series of signs for HORSHAM STEPS. Descend into the valley.

Cross the mossed boulders at Horsham Steps *with care*, especially after rain. (For an easier but longer way round by Foxworthy bridge, see sketch map.) Follow the path upstream along the bank, then right to a path junction. Turn right, HAMMERSLAKE FOR LUSTLEIGH. The path climbs gently to a small fork: keep right with the PATH sign. Turn left at the next path junction for HAMMERSLAKE.

Turn right through a gate at the next fingerpost. Reaching a lane, turn left and after 25 m turn right, PUBLIC FOOTPATH. Follow the pleasant woodland path to Lower Coombe. Turn right through a gate for LUSTLEIGH.

Ignore the next kissing gate and its side turning. Turn right at the next fingerpost after that (LUSTLEIGH VILLAGE INDIRECT) and take the downhill path. Turn left at the next gate and follow the brook, then cross it by a bridge of boulders and keep left at a path crossing.

Walk on to enter Lustleigh Orchard by a small gate. Continue past the May Queen's throne and the playground to the village centre.

Walk 6 Widecombe and Hameldown

Distance: 13 km (8¹/₄ miles)   Time: 4¹/₄ hours
Character: This exhilarating circuit offers some of Dartmoor's finest
views, especially from Hameldown (529 m above sea level). Be prepared
for some steep slopes, especially at the start. A Bronze Age walled village
with hut circles, medieval tin workings, mementos of the Second World
War and a characteristic longhouse add to the interest. High ground, so
map and compass needed for safety.
Pubs: The Rugglestone (01364) 621327; the Old Inn (01364) 621207.

Park in the car park opposite the church at Widecombe (SX719769).
Turn left out of the car park and follow the BOVEY TRACEY road for
200 m. Just before the bridge over the East Webburn River, turn left
into a lane. This soon climbs sharply and passes Middle Bonehill, a
sturdy granite and thatch longhouse dated 1683 on the lintel.

Continue steadily uphill. Emerging onto the open moor (where
there's a steep hill sign, in case you hadn't noticed it was steep!), turn
left onto a farm access track and 50m ahead bear right up the steep
flank of Bell Tor. Widecombe's tall church tower appears a mere toy in
the valley below. It is dwarfed by Hameldown, russet with bracken in
winter, purple with heather in late summer.

Keep to the right of Bell Tor, then head to the summit of Chinkwell
Tor and two modern cairns – though one is built on top of an ancient
cairn. Now follow the well-defined track down to the col between

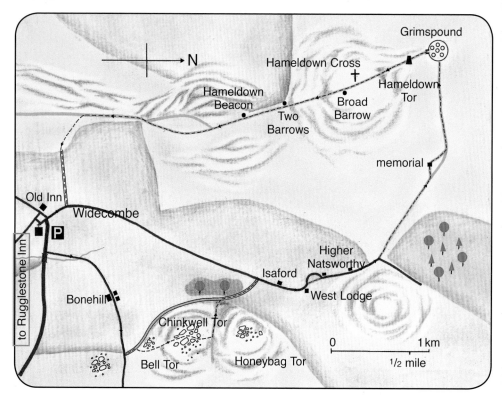

Chinkwell and Honeybag Tors. Turn left and downhill, following the path down to a track. Turn right and follow the track round and down to a metalled lane.

Turn right and follow the lane past Isaford and West Lodge. After another 200m, use the PATH on the right to cut out a dog-leg in the lane. Walk on and pass Higher Natsworthy Farm, then after another 400m turn left onto PUBLIC BRIDLEPATH ROAD NEAR FIRTH BRIDGE. Follow the broad path uphill, keeping the dry stone wall on your right. Stick to the path as it diverges to the left of the wall, and heads NW.

Just short of the summit is a granite memorial to four RAF crew, killed here when their bomber crashed in 1941. Turn right at the memorial, and then left onto a second broad path which leads over the brow of the hill and down to Grimspound.

This Bronze Age walled settlement covers 1.6 hectares and contains 24 restored hut circles, giving a vivid idea of the size and shape of our ancestors' houses. Distinctly defined on the hillside opposite are medieval tin workings and ancient field patterns.

Leave the settlement by the great gateway on the southern (uphill) side and take the path which climbs up to a triangulation pillar and cairn on Hameldown Tor. Continue ahead on the superb ridgeway

track past Hameldown Cross, Broad Barrow, Two Barrows and 'Hamilton Beacon'. Wonderful views of Honeybag, Chinkwell, Hay Tor and Rippon Tor open out.

The track eventually descends. Follow it down to the corner of a stone wall. Walk ahead (WIDECOMBE) with the wall on your left. After 400m, bear left and follow the path downhill and into an enclosed track, then a tarmac lane. Turn right at the T-junction, into Widecombe.

For the car park turn left. For the Old Inn turn right. Said to be 14th century and an inn since it was first built, it has been altered and added to over the years. However it retains three good stone fireplaces. There are oil paintings and period photographs of Widecombe. Enjoy the beer garden and the sun lounge in the summer.

Opposite the Old Inn is the 16th century Church House, which serves as the village shop, market venue and meeting centre. It is distinguished by its granite ashlar and its loggia.

To reach the RUGGLESTONE INN, cross the square and turn left. It is 400m away and can be reached on foot or by car. This small, friendly, locals' inn now offers food. Note the photographs of Widecombe Fair and the local hunt, and the 'vagging iron' for cutting peat turfs. Again, there are open fires and a good garden.

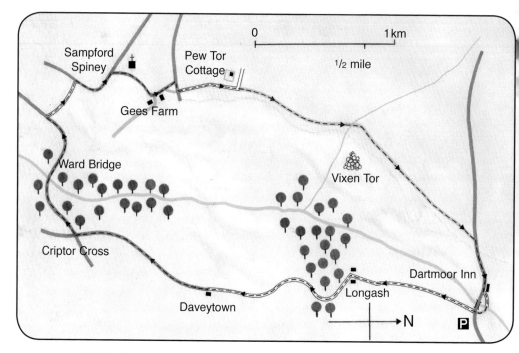

Walk 7   Merrivale and Sampford Spiney

Distance: 9.25 km (5³/4 miles)   Duration of walk: 2³/4 hours
Character: A fairly gentle Dartmoor walk by footpaths and quiet lanes,
with views of several tors and the delightful church of Sampford Spiney.

Park on the B3357 Tavistock-Princetown road in a small car park
500 m east of the Dartmoor Inn at Merrivale. Turn left and walk 250 m
downhill. Turn left in front of the cottages and walk through the metal
gate signed PLEASE KEEP TO TRACK. Walk on towards Longash. Walk
through the Longash yard, then walk ahead, keeping the stone wall on
your right.

Continue through a small oak wood and on to the tarred lane at
Daveytown. Follow the lane to Criptor Cross. Turn right for WARD
BRIDGE/WOODTOWN. Cross the bridge and walk uphill to a cattle-grid.
Bear right onto a track UNSUITABLE FOR MOTOR VEHICLES. On reach-
ing the tarred lane go straight on. When the lane forks, bear right.
Sampford Spiney church has a handsome and locally characteristic
Perpendicular tower with tall pinnacles.

From the church, continue up the same lane. Do not take the footpath at Gees Farm but walk on for a further 100 m and take the waymarked footpath on the right just beyond Eastontown. Cut across the
rough grass ahead to a lane. Continue up a track towards Pewtor

22

Cottage. The cottage is surrounded by a high hedge; where the track turns sharply left at the end of the hedge, walk ahead on a NNE bearing following a well beaten path which soon becomes a stony track. Follow this round a small disused quarry, where many of the stones bear the marks of quarrymen's tools. Keep the wall on your right. Walk to the left of the Vixen Tor enclosure. Vixen has the highest rock (28 m) of any Dartmoor tor, and is sometimes called 'the Sphinx' because of its shape.

Cross the brook and walk ahead, keeping the wall on your right.

On reaching the road turn right and follow the verge down past the Merrivale Quarry to the Dartmoor Inn,.

After refreshment, turn left out of the inn and follow the redundant section of old road to cross the River Walkham by the old turnpike road bridge. Retrace your steps to the car park.

The Dartmoor Inn

Tel: (01822) 890340. It was first recorded as an inn in 1841 when it was probably a coaching stop. It is made up of four or five 17th century cottages, though the dividing walls were removed forty years ago to make the long bar with wooden ceilings we see today. In the 1950s the fireplace was attractively enlarged with granite from the nearby quarry. Merrivale, the last sizeable Dartmoor granite quarry, was closed in the 1990s but stands behind the Inn as a stark reminder of what was one of the moor's main industries.

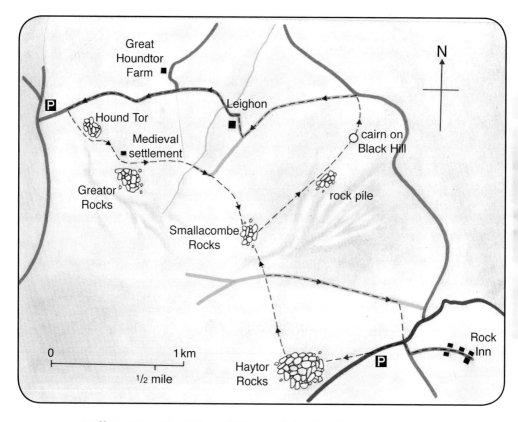

Walk 8 Hay Tor, Hound Tor and the Rock Inn

Length: 11.8 km (7 1/2 miles)   Duration of walk: 3 1/2 hours
Character: A walk combining great views with prehistoric and
industrial archaeology. Paths, quiet lanes and open moorland. Four
ascents and descents, some quite steep. Map and compass essential.

The Rock Inn

Tel: (01364) 661305. Built around 1826, along with the adjoining
quarrymen's cottages, by quarry and tramway owner George Templer,
the Rock was first a coaching inn, then a hotel. There are several
period photographs in the bar – the Rock is instantly recognisable.
There are also more recent photographs of Dartmoor life and people
by local photographer Chris Chapman. Enjoy the colourful garden in
summer, or in winter the log fire in the partly panelled bar, with its
antiques and polished tables.

Park at the main Hay Tor car park (SX 765772), with its National Park

information centre. Walk up the broad track to the summit of Haytor Rocks and enjoy the views, including Haldon, the Teign estuary, the South Hams and many Dartmoor tors.

Walk due north along a narrow path through the heather to cross the path of the granite tramway. Take the broad track that leads on to Smallacombe Rocks.

From Smallacombe Rocks, bear NE on the path through the heather leading to the rock pile on the brow of the hill. From the rock pile continue in the same direction to the cairn at the top of Black Hill, another wonderful viewpoint. Walk ahead downhill on a broad path through the heather, aiming for the point where a track below you joins a tarmac lane.

Turn left along the track (not the lane) and after 900 m turn right, signed BY-WAY FOR LEIGHON. Walk past Leighon House, cross a stream, and bear left signed ROAD TO GREAT HOUNDTOR. At a road junction, keep left. The road soon begins to climb.

To explore Hound Tor, walk on over the cattle grid and then to the car park. Turn left and walk up to the summit. Legends of demon hounds associated with these fantastic rock piles fed the imagination of Sir Arthur Conan Doyle when he visited Dartmoor, and added greatly to *The Hound of the Baskervilles*.

From the summit of Hound Tor walk SE down a broad grassy path to join the well-beaten path between Greator Rock and the fascinating remains of a medieval hamlet, one of 130 such settlements on Dartmoor and one of five to have been excavated. A farmstead, barns, pens, five longhouses and ancillary buildings are clearly outlined.

Follow the path to a gate on the left of Greator Rocks – PUBLIC BRIDLEPATH LEIGHON VIA HAYTOR DOWN. The path descends steeply to a pretty clapper bridge. Walk on to a path junction. Do not turn left to Leighon, but continue uphill on an unsigned path. Follow this as it bears right near the top of the ridge and back to Smallacombe Rocks. This was a prehistoric settlement, and, bracken permitting, you should be able to find four impressive hut circles. (Prehistoric houses are generally round, medieval houses rectangular.)

Retrace your steps towards Haytor Rocks, but on reaching the tramway turn left along it and follow it eastward for 1.2 km. Then turn right down a path leading to the road near a red phone box.

Cross the road and head for HAYTOR VALE, over the cattle grid. Turn left for ROCK INN and walk down to it.

Retrace you steps uphill to the cattle grid and follow the road left (WIDECOMBE) to the car park.

Walk 9   Princetown, South Hessary Tor and Black Tor

Distance: 12.5 km (7 3/4 miles)   Duration of walk: 4 hours
Character: A moorland and forest walk, mainly by defined paths. It is
less steep than most moorland routes, and has much of historical
interest as well as magnificent views.

Turn right out of Princetown car park (SX 589735). Walk past the
National Park Visitor Centre and take the bridleway ahead, to the left
of a large slate-hung building. It is a flat, broad path leading to South
Hessary Tor, which has the stump of a Victorian spike on its crown.
This is a boundary marker for Dartmoor Forest, one of only two left.

   Walk on for another 1.6 km to a very clear junction of bridleways.
Turn right and head SW. Follow the track over the Devonport Leat at
Older Bridge and on by the old tin workings, the scars now covered
by grass and furze. Walk on to Newleycombe Cross, just to the left of
the track at SX 592703. This ancient cross, one of over a hundred on
Dartmoor, has been well restored. The original top portion has been
set in a new shaft, using the ancient socket stone.

   Continue along the track, enjoying the views of Sheeps Tor and
Burrator Reservoir. Enter woodland and turn right then left at a junction of tracks, PUBLIC BRIDLEPATH LEATHER TOR BRIDGE. Continue
descending to Leather Tor Bridge: turn right across the bridge and
start to ascend.

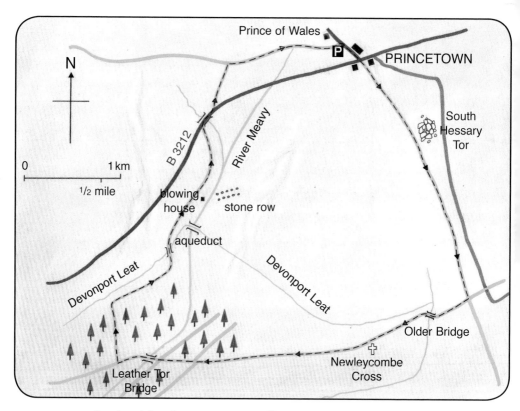

On the right after 150 m you will see a man-made cave, said to have been used by miners for storing potatoes: they stayed out here all the working week, far from their homes. 20 m beyond the cave, turn right over a stile for DEVONPORT LEAT. At the leat turn right, for STANLAKE FARM. Follow the path beside the leat and out of the woods by a gate.

Work began on the leat in 1793. It served the expanding community on the Devonport dockyard site until the construction of the Burrator Reservoir in 1898. Now diverted into Burrator, much of the leat remains as an integral part of local drainage. Trout abound.

Walk beside the leat and after 150 m cross by a clapper bridge. Continue upstream on the west bank to an aqueduct, which brings the leat down Raddick Hill, making a mini waterfall. Leave the leat here and follow the same NNE course along the path parallel to the infant River Meavy.

Follow the grassy path up, then bear right, nearing the river again, to Black Tor Falls and the ruins of a 17th century tin mill, marked 'Blowing House' on the OS map, because the waterwheel drove bellows which heated a furnace to smelt the ore. For centuries tin was the main source of Dartmoor's wealth. Although production peaked in

Tudor times, the industry continued into the early 20th century. The remains of trenches and mines are scattered all over the moor.

Continue up the west bank of the river. About 150 m beyond the blowing house ruins, on the opposite bank, you can see the Hart Tor double stone row, which is accessible in dry weather. It is 126 m long and ends at a cairn. A second cairn heads a shorter single row.

Continue more or less parallel to the river, but keep to the higher rougher ground along a rather indistinct path which runs between the tussocks of boggy ground and the slope of the hill on the left.

On meeting the Princetown Road, turn right across the bridge and after 50 m turn left into a rough path, aligning yourself a little to the right of the TV mast on North Hessary Tor.

Reaching the trackbed of the old railway, turn right and follow the path back to Princetown, where you will find the Prince of Wales pub and several cafés and tea-rooms.

The Prince of Wales

Princetown was only established in the 1780s by Sir Thomas Tyrwhitt as a pioneering agricultural settlement and named in honour of his friend the Prince of Wales, later King George IV. It is thus a newer settlement than Princeton, New Jersey, which was first named in 1724, probably after King William III, Prince of Orange. The Prince of Wales Inn (01822 890219) has log fires and a superb collection of local photographs, giving a vivid impression of life in Princetown.

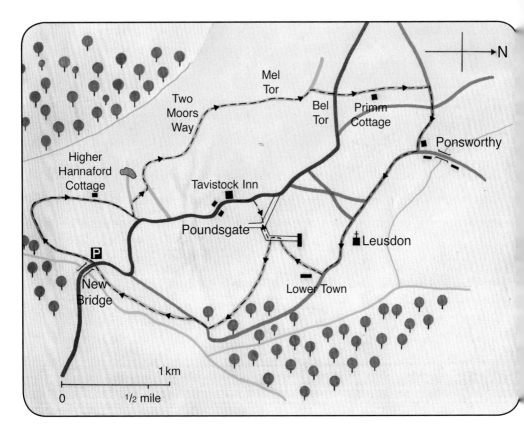

Walk 10 New Bridge, Dr Blackall's Drive and the Tavistock Inn

Distance: 11.8km (7¹/₂ miles) including a diversion to Mel Tor.
Duration of walk: 4 hours
Character: A combination of beautiful moorland, woodland and
riverside walking along footpaths and quiet lanes. There are splendid
views of both the deeply eroded Dart valley and the surrounding tors.

Start from the car park (SX 711709) by New Bridge – which is in fact medieval. Walk upriver along the minor lane from the back of the car park. Stay with the lane as it diverges from the Dart. Continue uphill past the Hannaford Farms.

About 1.35km (³/₄ mile) from the start, a stony track joins the road from the left: turn sharp left onto this – heading towards a disused quarry – and then after 100m bear right uphill to meet a broad track.

Turn left and follow this track (marked Two Moors Way and Dr Blackall's Drive on the OS map) for 2.5km. It is fairly level because it was designed as a carriage drive in Victorian times by Dr Blackall for his invalid wife, to enable her to enjoy the vistas.

30

Beyond Mel Tor Tor (a short diversion left and a wonderful view-point) the track continues between stone walls. When it divides, turn 90° right and follow the stone wall up to the road at Bel Tor Corner.

Cross over and continue ahead on the well-beaten path. Keep right down towards Primm Cottage, then follow the track to the left of the enclosure. At the end of the enclosure keep left and walk ahead on a rough track to a tarred lane.

Turn right and walk past Looksgate Cross downhill to the ford at Ponsworthy. Cross by a clapper bridge. Turn right and walk on for 1 km. Bear left for LEUSDON CHURCH/LOWER TOWN. Pass the church and continue downhill for 350 m to a red post box on the right.

Turn right here and follow the track to a wooden gate with a yellow sign. Walk on through fields as signed, keeping the hedge on your right. On reaching a lane, turn left. The next path junction has a tall fingerpost.

To visit the Tavistock Inn turn right up the lane. Keep right, into an avenue, then turn left through a spiky metal gate (PATH) beside a leat. Turn left onto the road, which can be busy, but the pub is only 250 m along it.

On leaving the pub, retrace your steps to the tall fingerpost. Cross a stile and keep the hedge on your left. On reaching Great Wood, fork left down the broad track (waymarked) to a tarred lane. Turn right and take the next turning right.

Follow the lane alongside the river, past the handsome lodge of Spitchwick Manor, until the lane diverts from the bank. Walk ahead across the meadow, keeping the river on your left. This is a fine bathing place in summer and ablaze with colour in the autumn, but most dramatic when the Dart is in spate. Walk on to New Bridge.

The Tavistock Inn

Tel: (01364) 631251. Medieval in origin, the Tavistock gets its name from being on the Ashburton to Tavistock Road. It is thought to have been a farmhouse before it became specialised as an inn, which is not uncommon – travellers in remote areas used to rely on roadside farms for their refreshment. Its ancient stone staircase is remarkable. Enjoy the beer garden with its flowers, or the comfortable bar with its log fires, according to the season.

Trust you won't meet the Devil, who is said to have popped in one Sunday in 1638 on his way to destroy Widecombe Church by fire and thunder. The beer sizzled in his throat. He left scorch marks on the bar, and the seventeenth century equivalent of a bouncing cheque – his money turned to dry leaves as soon as he left!

Walk 11 Hexworthy and Dartmeet

Length: 11 km (6¾ miles)   Duration of walk: 3¼ hours
Character: Field and moorland paths, bridleways and quiet lanes. The
views are magnificent. There is one steep ascent.
NB The second half of the walk has stepping stones and should not be
attempted after heavy rain. Parts of the route are wet underfoot.

The Forest Inn

Tel (01364) 631211 (to check parking availability)
www.theforestinn.co.uk

The Forest Inn enjoys a splendid situation in the midst of Dartmoor's
grandest scenery. It was a favourite haunt of Dartmoor author William
Crossing, who knew the old thatched building before it was ravaged by
fire. The inn as we see it was completed in 1916 and bears the Prince
of Wales' symbol – a plume of three feathers. Inside is a restaurant,
easy chairs and an open fire, as well as Dartmoor landscape paintings.
and a good collection of local photographs. Walkers are welcome.

Parking opposite the inn (SW655726) is reserved for customers.
Otherwise, park carefully off-road on the lane leading uphill from the
inn, or use the small parking area 500 m along the lane branching right
from this towards Sherberton. Alternatively, start from the Dartmeet
car park.

Take the lane in front of the inn and follow it down to Hexworthy
and then up. Immediately after Thimble Hall, turn left and walk

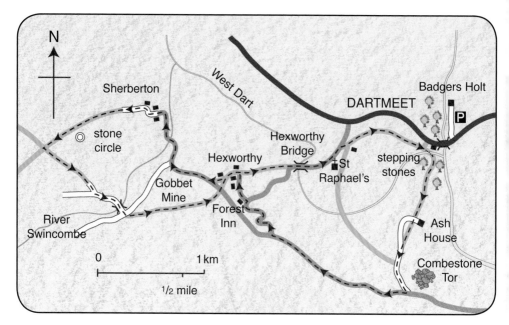

uphill. Cross a tarmac access drive, then after 80 m join a lane. Turn right to go over a cattle grid and follow the lane down. On the left are the remains of the 19th century Gobbet Mine and a little further up the valley are the remains of older tin works.

Cross the bridge and walk up to Sherberton Farm. Take the BRIDLEWAY between the farm buildings; turn left in front of the saw-yard into an enclosed track. Continue through the next gate onto the open moor.

Follow the BRIDLEWAY sign ahead, keeping the wall and fence on your left. The stone circle in the far left corner of the field is worth seeing, though most of its stones have been lost to the nearby wall. Don't take the gate here, but walk uphill for a further 150 m, keeping the wall on your left.

Leave the field by the gate and follow the well-beaten path to a junction. Turn left. After 600 m cross the stile at the end of the field, and after 60 m keep left, following the BRIDLEPATH to a footbridge. Cross over and walk ahead, signed BRIDLEPATH. Continue to the lane, cross over and retrace your steps to Thimble Hall.

Either visit the inn now, or turn left opposite Thimble Hall on the PUBLIC FOOTPATH for the second loop of this walk. Go through the yard ahead and into the field. Follow the path sign and cross the stone stile at the far end of the field. Walk down to the tarred lane, cross Hexworthy Bridge and walk on to St Raphael's Church. Built in 1869

to serve this part of the huge Lydford parish, it was also used as a school. The children's desks are now pews – with inkwell holders still in evidence.

Take the next turning right, opposite Huccaby Farm. Do not take the gate in front of you but bear left uphill through a gate signed DARTMOOR WAY with a warning about the stepping stones. Walk ahead following the yellow waymarks over the hill and down into an enclosed lane.

The path leads into a field and down to a house. Follow the lane behind the house to visit Dartmeet, where Badgers Holt offers refreshments. The road bridge here is dated 1792 and belongs to the turnpike era: upstream a few metres is its predecessor, a clapper bridge which may be medieval in origin.

Retrace your steps to the path. Turn left, PUBLIC BRIDLEWAY COMBESTONE. Cross the stepping stones carefully. On the far bank, take the path uphill through trees (NB not the riverbank path). Reaching Ash House, walk ahead, then join a farm track. Continue on this track at the next junction.

On reaching the road, turn left to visit Combestone Tor, a fine granite pile showing characteristic horizontal weathering and a rock basin. Turn right onto the lane and follow it down over the bridge, then up again. Fork right (PRINCETOWN 6) when the road divides and walk down to the Forest Inn.

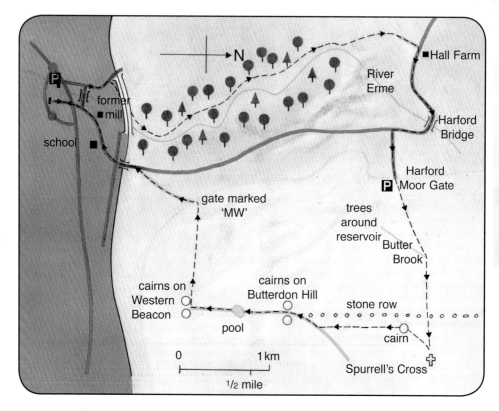

Walk 12 Ivybridge, Harford and Spurrell's Cross

Distance: 12.2 km (7³/4 miles) Duration of walk: 4¹/4 hours
Character: A beautiful bankside path along the fast flowing Erme, then
a quiet lane to Harford and onto the open moor (compass and OS map
needed for safety). Ancient monuments and superb views.

Start from the town centre car parks in Ivybridge (SX 637561) where
the Leonards Road section has long-stay parking. Walk down to the
river (away from the ring-road) and turn right upriver along the path
and past a terrace. At the road junction, go forward into Harford Road
past a short-stay car park with a 1937 water turbine.

Turn left over the Erme by a small high-arched bridge. Turn right
into Station Road and walk past the former Stowford Paper Mill. Take
the PUBLIC FOOTPATH by an information board. Walk under the 1893
railway viaduct. The granite piers of Brunel's original 1848 timber
viaduct stand behind.

Follow the bankside path for the next 2.3 km, ignoring the three
PATH signs on the left. Continue over stiles and a duckboard to a
fourth PATH sign. Follow it left away from the river and thence uphill to
a path junction. Turn right through a wooden gate as signed. Follow a

36

series of PATH signs through the wood. Keep left when the path forks. Turn right into a field as signed and walk across the next field to join a track to the left of a dry stone wall. Keep right over a brook and through a gate.

On reaching the tarmac lane, turn right and walk on to Harford Church. Leave by the south gate. Turn left and uphill past the School House to Harford Moor Gate. Continue in the same direction (ENE) over open ground. Cross the Butter Brook near the top of its little valley and head for a low mound on the skyline ahead, which looks like a barrow but isn't one. Just before you reach it you will cross a path beside the Butterdon Hill stone row – 2 km long, the second longest on the moor. Carry on ENE, crossing a disused railway track, and after about 300 m you should see Spurrell's Cross – not immediately visible but just over a brow of rising ground.

From the cross, head SSW across rough grass and heather for 150 m. At the top of the slope you will find a cairn (at SX 658598). Now aim for the large cairns on Butterdon Hill to the south: you will pick up a broad grassy track leading to them, and to a triangulation pillar. From the pillar, take the track south towards Western Beacon, following a line of boundary stones and passing a pool.

From the cairns on the Western Beacon, turn west, aiming for the point at which two lines of trees intersect. Follow the broad grassy path down to a wooden gate marked MW (Two Moors Way). Take this track down to a tarmac lane. Turn left. Cross the railway bridge and walk ahead past a No Entry sign. Follow the road past the school and the former paper mill towards the town centre, where you might like to divert left to visit the Trehill Arms on Harford Road or the Sportsman's Inn on Exeter Road.

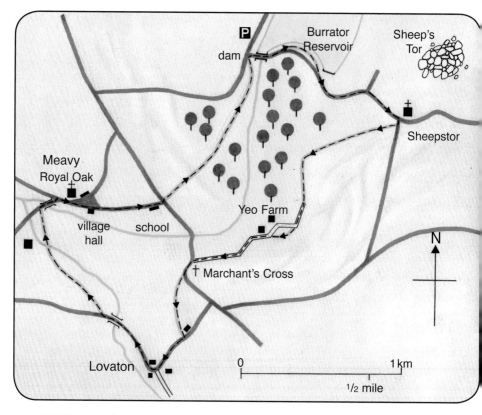

Walk 13   Sheepstor and Meavy

Distance: 7km (4½ miles)   Duration of walk: 2¼ hours
*Character: A gentle moorland edge walk through fields and woods, with
lovely views of Burrator Reservoir and surrounding moorland.*
*Two historic churches, three ancient crosses and a fine old inn add to
the interest.*

Park on the roadside at the western end of Burrator Reservoir's dam
(SX 551680). Walk along the dam and enjoy the view north to
Sharpitor. Finished with granite blocks in 1898 and a triumph of
Victorian engineering, the dam has now melded beautifully into the
landscape.

   Walk ahead across the dam. Go through a gate on your left and follow the bankside path to the second dam. Rejoin the lane and continue to Sheepstor village. When the lane divides, keep right towards
the 15th century granite church. It has many interesting features
including a rood screen and carved bench ends. There is a memorial
to Sir James Brooke, the first White Rajah of Sarawak, who is buried
here with the other two White Rajahs. Their story is told in some

detail. Just south of the graveyard is a grassy area, once used as a bull-ring. The iron ring to which the baited bull was tethered was found here in a granite block.

Take the narrow lane opposite the ancient stone cross (restored in 1911) by the western entrance to the churchyard. Cross over the brook and 50 m ahead turn right, PUBLIC FOOTPATH MARCHANT'S CROSS. Cut diagonally across the first field, then follow the yellow waymarks, keeping near the wall on your right.

Cross a stone stile and enter an oak wood – full of bluebells in May. Climb down a ladder stile at the far end of the wood and turn right into an enclosed path. Follow the stiles and footpath signs around Yeo Farm (you are diverted to the left of the farm track). Bear left, signed PATH, along a tarmac track to Marchant's Cross.

At 2.4 m, Marchant's is the tallest of Dartmoor's old stone crosses and is 13th century or earlier. It served as a boundary marker between Meavy and Sheepstor parishes and probably marked and sanctified the Plympton Track between Tavistock Abbey and Plympton Priory.

Turn left and uphill for 150 m. Leave the road by a high stile, PUBLIC FOOTPATH. Cut diagonally across fields (noting the upright stone in the second – another waymark on the ancient track?) to emerge on a lane at Cole Cottage. Turn right down the lane, past a telephone box.

Cross the brook and after 80 m turn right at a stile, PUBLIC FOOTPATH. Follow the footpath signs. Cross the brook by a small stone clapper

bridge. Bear slightly left and join a track. Then go through a gate into an enclosed path. On reaching the lane, turn right and right again for Meavy.

The Meavy Oak stands on the village green. The local tradition is that this oak dates to the time of King John (1199-1216) and connects it with the original Norman church, consecrated in 1122. However, one recent researcher suggested it probably dates from AD 1039. Next to the oak are St Peter's, a largely 15th century granite church, and the Royal Oak.

Walk eastward from the oak, past the village hall and on towards the school, where a replica of Drake's Drum stands in a glass case in the wall. Turn left for DOUSLAND and almost immediately right onto the PUBLIC FOOTPATH. Follow the footpath by trees and through two wooden gates. When it divides, take the left path uphill through the trees to reach a leat marked PCWW 1917. Continue along the leat to the next fork. Bear left there, uphill to the dam.

The Royal Oak, Meavy

Tel: (01822) 852944. Like many Devon inns, this began as a church house. Built of stone and cob, the Royal Oak was also used by monks travelling between their establishments at Buckfast, Plympton and Tavistock. Inside the right-hand bar is a cavernous log fire and a range of period and modern maps and photographs showing village life. A sketch of 1810 shows the inn as it was then, and a document of 1588/9 mentions it.